# At Issue

## Invasive Species

# Other Books in the At Issue Series

# At Issue

# Invasive Species

*Noah Berlatsky, Book Editor*

**GREENHAVEN PRESS**
*A part of Gale, Cengage Learning*

GALE
CENGAGE Learning·

Farmington Hills, Mich • Sanfrancisco • New York • Waterville, Maine
Meriden, Conn • Mason, Ohio • Chicago

Judy Galens, *Manager, Frontlist Acquisitions*

© 2016 Greenhaven Press, a part of Gale, Cengage Learning.

Gale and Greenhaven Press are registered trademarks used herein under license.

*For more information, contact:*
Greenhaven Press
27500 Drake Rd.
Farmington Hills, MI 48331-3535
Or you can visit our Internet site at gale.cengage.com

For product information and technology assistance, contact us at

Gale Customer Support, 1-800-877-4253
For permission to use material from this text or product, submit all requests online at www.cengage.com/permissions.

Further permissions questions can be e-mailed to permissionrequest@cengage.com.

Articles in Greenhaven Press anthologies are often edited for length to meet page requirements. In addition, original titles of these works are changed to clearly present the main thesis and to explicitly indicate the author's opinion. Every effort is made to ensure that Greenhaven Press accurately reflects the original intent of the authors. Every effort has been made to trace the owners of copyrighted material.

Cover photograph copyright © Debra Hughes 2007. Used under license from Shutterstock.com.

**LIBRARY OF CONGRESS CATALOGING-IN-PUBLICATION DATA**

Names: Berlatsky, Noah, editor.
Title: Invasive species / Noah Berlatsky, book editor.
Description: Farmington Hills, Mich : Greenhaven Press, a part of Gale, Cengage Learning, [2016] | Series: At issue | Includes bibliographical references and index.
Identifiers: LCCN 2015024201| ISBN 9780737773866 (hardcover) | ISBN 9780737773873 (pbk.)
Subjects: LCSH: Nonindigenous pests. | Biological invasions. | Introduced organisms--Ecology. | Animal introduction. | Climatic changes.
Classification: LCC QH353 .I58269 2016 | DDC 344.04/6--dc23
LC record available at http://lccn.loc.gov/2015024201

Printed in Mexico
1 2 3 4 5 6 7 19 18 17 16 15

# Contents

# Introduction

At first, it might seem strange to consider the coyote an invasive species in the United States. After all, the animal is native to North America. However, while coyotes may be native to the southwest, they can now be found in most parts of the eastern continent, as their range has expanded noticeably, and surprisingly, in recent times. For example, in the 1980s, coyotes in Florida moved from living in eighteen counties to roaming throughout forty-eight counties in the state. In Canada, the coyote moved into Ontario at the beginning of the twentieth century, into Quebec in the 1940s, and all the way to Canada's eastern provinces in the 1970s.

When coyotes move into new habitats, they are often considered invasive species. Like many successful invasive species, coyotes thrive in their new territories. The coyote has startled scientists and biologists, especially, with its success in urban areas. Researchers who studied coyotes in the Chicago, Illinois, metropolitan area in the early 2000s expected to discover only isolated individuals. Instead, they found a large and diverse population, numbering between several hundred and a few thousand.

"We couldn't find an area in Chicago where there weren't coyotes," said researcher Stan Gehrt. "They've learned to exploit all parts of their landscape."[1] Coyotes were in parks, but they also lived in industrial parks and around residential and commercial buildings. In addition, coyotes in urban areas seemed to live longer than coyotes in rural areas. Urban coyotes had a 60 percent chance of living for a year, which was twice as high as a rural coyote's chance of living for that amount of time. In short, coyotes—like many "invasives"—

---

1. Quoted in Holly Wagner, "On the Loose: Urban Coyotes Thrive in North American Cities," Ohio State Research, January 3, 2005. http://researchnews.osu.edu/archive /urbcoyot.htm.

seem to do better in their new homes than they did in their old ones. And this was not just in Chicago. Los Angeles, Boston, and New York all also have substantial coyote populations.

Like other invasives, coyotes can be expensive and can harm the local ecology. In rural areas, especially, coyotes can do significant damage to livestock and agriculture. A 2004 nationwide survey of livestock and poultry producers found that coyotes had killed more than 135,000 sheep and lambs at a cost of $10.7 million. As a result, the federal government spends millions of dollars trapping and poisoning up to 90,000 coyotes a year. Coyotes also can kill household pets if they are allowed to wander outside in suburban or rural areas—or even in cities.[2]

But while the coyotes demonstrate the downsides of invasive species, they have some positive benefits as well. They occupy the top of the food chain; with wolves, bobcats, bears, and other animals largely absent, coyotes serve as the main predator in urban ecologies. Coyotes in Chicago, for example, eat goose eggs, and are therefore an important brake on populations of Canadian geese. Geese can themselves be a pest; flocks of them may destroy grass and leave large quantities of droppings behind. Geese populations were growing at 10 to 20 percent per year in Chicago before the coyotes arrived. The coyotes slowed that growth to only 1 or 2 percent. Coyotes may also help to control populations of rabbits and rats in urban areas.

Those who live in urban areas rarely see coyotes—which is not an accident. Coyotes are nocturnal and rarely encounter or bother humans. From 1960 to 2006, there were a total of 159 coyote bites reported. In contrast, Cook County, which contains Chicago, had five thousand domestic dog bites in

---

2. Bruce Watson, "10 Invasive Species That Cost the U.S. a Bundle," *DailyFinance*, August 25, 2010. www.dailyfinance.com/2010/08/25/10-invasive-species-that-cost-the-u-s-a-bundle.

2012 alone. Coyotes thrive in urban areas in part because they avoid humans; they don't hurt people and so are in general not targeted for extermination. In contrast, in rural areas, where coyotes go after livestock, they are hunted as pests (which perhaps explains part of why coyote life expectancy in urban areas is longer).

So, if coyotes in eastern urban areas don't bother humans and fill an important ecological niche, should they really be considered invasive pests? Science writer Fred Pearce has argued that alarmist reaction to the coyote, and species like the coyote, suggests that the antipathy to invasives is flawed. Instead, he argues, thriving invasives are nature's way of trying to right ecologies thrown out of balance by human intervention. "The more damage that humans do to nature—through climate change, pollution, and grabbing land for intensive agriculture and plantation forestry—the more important alien species and novel ecosystems will be to ensuring nature's survival," Pearce argues. "Aliens are rapidly changing from being part of the problem to part of the solution." Coyotes, he says, are part of "the new wild"—a species that manages to fit into the landscape and ecology humans have created.[3]

The rest of *At Issue: Invasive Species* looks at other controversies surrounding invasive species, including questions of how to control invasives, which species qualify as invasives, and whether invasives are good or bad for the environment.

---

3. Fred Pearce, "Invasive Species Will Save Us: The New Way We Must Think About the Environment Now," *Salon*, April 11, 2015. www.salon.com/2015/04/11/invasive _species_will_save_us_the_new_way_we_must_think_about_the_environment_now/.

# 1

# Invasive Species Do Not Always Harm the Environment

*Cord Riechelmann*

*Cord Riechelmann is a writer at DW, a German broadcaster and media organization.*

*In most cases, invasive species do little damage to native wildlife. For example, raccoons introduced into Germany did no harm to local species. The one exception is island ecosystems, where introduced species can cause great harm. However, the best response is usually to work to preserve native species rather than to eliminate introduced ones, since eliminating invasive species once they take hold is almost impossible.*

When Christopher Columbus reached America in 1492, he ushered in what can be considered a new era in biology. Ships and boats sailing the world's oceans have been transporting animals and plants from continent to continent on an unprecedented scale. In parts of the San Francisco Bay, where various ships have sailed for centuries, 99 percent of the flora and fauna are exotic. By exotic, I mean that these species are native to Africa, Europe or Asia, but not America. These species include birds like the European starling (*Sturnus vulgaris*) and the house sparrow (*Passer domesticus*).

The picture isn't much different here in Europe as the evolutionary biologist and ecologist Josef H. Reichholf describes in his book *A Short Natural History of the Last Millennium*: "Time and again, the conditions shifted through periods of warmer and colder climates, but in Central Europe, the climatic transition zone between the 'Atlantic West' and the 'Continental East' in particular remained a mixed area for flora and fauna with an apparently large capacity to take in (new species)."

Looking at the last 300 years alone, the loss of species would have been disastrous if new and foreign populations were separated from the native ones. That would mean that nearly all orchid species would disappear, as would the leafy chestnut trees that provide shade in our backyards and beer gardens.

## A Bad Reputation

While the movement to stamp out orchids or chestnut trees never materialized, the Chinese mitten crab (*Eriocheir sinensis*) and the North American raccoon (*Procyon lotor*) weren't so lucky. When they started to multiply in Germany in the 20th century, everyone started sounding the alarm. It was feared that the crab and raccoon, both omnivores, would literally rob native species of their food. But nothing of the sort happened. With both creatures, there was never any proof that they threatened the local flora and fauna. There weren't even the slightest signs that they had increased the competition. Apparently, the American raccoon and the Chinese mitten crab had squirreled their way into areas that weren't really being used. Still, it wasn't a completely smooth transition.

Mitten crabs burrow into river banks and spend their entire adult lives in embankments and dykes. But that means they can disrupt and even destroy important river defense systems. Raccoons, on the other hand, can wreak havoc when they intrude in people's homes. They are remarkably skilled at getting through doors and windows and into shelves, and they can leave a trail of destruction behind them. In both cases, it is human beings—not other animals—that suffer the consequences. On large landmasses like the U.S. or Europe, the majority of new species don't seem to cause much of a problem. In America, there were no signs that the European starling and the house sparrow had a negative effect on the local bird populations.

## Small Island, Big Problem

But when it comes to small islands, it's a different story. Guam is a good example of the effect of invasive species on an island. Ever since the brown tree snake (*Boiga irregularis*) arrived in Guam, native bird species have all but disappeared. The snake has no natural enemies on the island and ideal living conditions, especially because the local bird populations didn't know how to react to predatory snakes.

*Protecting species is not about fighting what's already a losing battle against invasive foreign flora and fauna: it's an effort to educate and preserve what's already there.*

The effect on Guam has been particularly dramatic because there simply isn't any cure. People there have to live with the snakes, which, for their part, don't seem to have any problem with human civilization. For example, scientists even discovered crumpled pieces of plastic wrap that were used to package raw hamburgers in the serpents' stomachs. So the brown tree snake can feed off the contents of our refrigerators.

The results are already comparable to the arrival of rats on Mauritius some four hundred years ago. Those rats managed to push the Dodo, a one-meter large flightless bird, into extinction because it didn't have any way to defend its nests from the versatile predators—and it will be the same story for most of Guam's bird species.

The only way to preserve the rest of the native birds is to protect certain species, in a very careful and targeted way. And that can only work if you educate and involve the local population on the island. So protecting species is not about fighting what's already a losing battle against invasive foreign flora and fauna: it's an effort to educate and preserve what's already there.

# 2

# Eradicating Invasive Species May Be Ecologically Harmful

*Katrina Voss*

*Katrina Voss is a writer for Penn State Science.*

*Invasive species are often seen as dangerous for native wildlife. However, a recent scientific study found that honeysuckle grow-ing in Pennsylvania actually benefited native bird species by pro-viding them with a source of food. Native plant species also ben-efited, since birds transferred seeds from both honeysuckle and native plants. The scientists concluded that in some cases inva-sive species might fill important ecological niches and could help other wildlife thrive.*

Ateam of scientists has discovered that human-introduced, invasive species of plants can have positive ecological ef-fects. Tomás Carlo, an assistant professor of biology at Penn State University, and Jason Gleditsch, a graduate student in the Department of Biology, have studied how invasive fruiting plants affect ecosystems and how those effects, contrary to prevailing ideas, sometimes can be beneficial to an ecological community. The team's research, which will be published in the journal *Diversity and Distributions*, is expected to affect the way environmental resource managers respond to ecosys-tem maintenance.

## More Harm than Good
## Through Eradication

"Among conservation biologists, ecologists, and managers, the default approach is to try to eliminate and root out non-native, invasive shrubs—anything that seems to change an ecosystem," Carlo said. "The fundamental goal is to return a natural area to its original, pristine state, with the native species occupying the dominant position in the community. But the problem is that most native communities already have been changed beyond recognition by humans, and many native species are now rare." Carlo explained that his team wanted to test whether certain well-established, invasive fruiting species have negative or positive effects on bird and fruiting-plant communities. "We wondered: Are we sometimes doing more harm than good when we eradicate plants that, despite being introduced recently, have formed positive relationships with native animals?" To be considered invasive, a species of plant must have been introduced by humans, and it must be dominant numerically in the new environment.

*It's a win-win-win for all three: the birds, the honeysuckle, and the nightshades.*

To test the impact of an invasive fruiting-plant species on native bird communities, Carlo and Gleditsch sectioned off an area of central Pennsylvania known as the Happy Valley region, where honeysuckle—a non-native fruiting plant that is considered invasive—grows in abundance. They then assessed the abundance of bird species and fruiting plants—including honeysuckle—within the area. After comparing their data with similar data from urban, agricultural, and forested areas, they determined that the abundance of honeysuckle predicted the numbers and diversity of birds within the region and even beyond the region. That is, the honeysuckle and bird communities had formed a relationship known as mutualism—a term

15

that describes how two or more species interact by benefiting mutually from each other's existence.

"The abundance of fruit-eating birds in the Happy Valley region is linked to the abundance of honeysuckle," Carlo explained. "Honeysuckle comprises more than half of all the fruits available in the landscape, and it benefits birds by providing them with a source of food in the fall. Meanwhile, birds benefit honeysuckle by dispersing the plant's seeds across a wider geographical area, helping the species to occupy more and more territory in areas already affected by human activities." Carlo explained that returning this particular ecosystem to its honeysuckle-free state could harm many species of native birds that now seem to rely on honeysuckle as a major food source in the fall.

The team also tested the honeysuckle's influence, not just on birds, but on other species of fruiting plants. First, they grew native fruiting plants known as American nightshades in pots in a greenhouse. When the fruits were ripe on each plant, they then placed them into both honeysuckle-dense areas and areas area without honeysuckle but dominated by other native and non-native fruiting species. "We chose the American nightshade because it is native and common in the Happy Valley region," Carlo said. "Also, it is easy to manipulate experimentally, and its fruits are eaten—and thus dispersed—by native birds."

## Birds Thrive with Invasives

In the area in which honeysuckle grew in abundance, the rate of fruit-removal of Carlo's American nightshades was 30-percent higher than in the areas without honeysuckle. Carlo explained that in the honeysuckle-rich area, birds were present in abundance. These birds allowed the nightshades to receive more seed-dispersal services—an ecological process known as facilitation. "The newly introduced plants piggybacked on the success of the honeysuckle, which is a common phenomenon because fruit-eating birds usually feed on a variety of fruit—whatever happens to be available to them," Carlo explained. "The same birds that ate the honeysuckle also ate the American nightshade, dispersing the seeds of both plants. It's a win-win-win for all three: the birds, the honeysuckle, and the nightshades."

Carlo also explained that in Pennsylvania there are now three to four times more fruit-eating birds such as robins and catbirds than there were just 30 years ago, especially in landscapes of high human presence. So scientists should conclude that, while some invasive, human-introduced plants are definitely problematic, others could serve to restore ecological balance by providing essential food resources to native migratory birds that populate areas affected by humans. "Invasive species could fill niches in degraded ecosystems and help restore native biodiversity in an inexpensive and self-organized way that requires little or no human intervention," Carlo said.

In addition, Carlo explained, while eliminating an invasive species could result in harm to the newly formed balance of an ecosystem, large-scale attempts to remove species also could be a waste of time and tax dollars. He explained that when managers and agencies attempt to eradicate an invasive plant from a particular ecosystem, the species often ends up growing back anyway. "Nature is in a constant state of flux, always shifting and readjusting as new relationships form between species, and not all of these relationships are bad just because they are novel or created by humans," Carlo said. "We need to be more careful about shooting first and asking questions later—assuming that introduced species are inherently harmful. We should be asking: Are we responding to real threats to nature or to our cultural perception and scientific bias?"

# 3

# Eating Invasive Species Can Help Reduce Their Impact

*Nancy Matsumoto*

*Nancy Matsumoto is a journalist who writes about art, culture, food, and Japanese-American culture for various publications.*

*Invasive species like snakehead fish, feral pigs, and Canada geese can all be prepared and eaten by humans. Many chefs are specializing in serving invasives. It can be difficult to create widespread, rather than local, markets for invasives, in part because of supply and distribution problems, and in part because people aren't used to eating these creatures. However, over time, it is hoped that increased consumption of invasives can reduce their number, or at least raise awareness of their ecological dangers.*

Austin Murphy likes to hunt snakehead fish on the tidal waters of the Potomac River. The fish, native to China, have earned local renown for their horror flick-like ability to breathe air and survive for short periods on land, their sharp teeth, and their thick, mucus-secreting skin. They're voracious carnivores with no known predators except humans and are all too at home in their adopted waters. Hunting them in the shallow, aquatic-plant-choked mouths of creeks and tributaries is tricky work, most easily done at night with a light and archery gear, though some fishermen prefer the more challenging method of daytime fly fishing. If the conditions are right, a skilled hunter can bag 200 pounds of snakehead in a summer season outing, says Murphy.

# Eat the Invaders

Snakeheads are just one example of "invasives" muscling in on native species, hogging resources and decimating land, seas and crops to the tune of over $120 billion a year. An avid fisherman and hunter, he's out for pleasure, but also to promote recreational snakehead hunting as a means to both help the environment and procure dinner. Snakehead, he says, "is excellent table fare." He filets them, seasons them with Old Bay, salt and pepper, then grills them right on the boat. Or, he says, "If I'm making sandwiches, I'll make starches and vegetables ahead. The fish is the star."

Although the impact of snakeheads on the environment is still being studied, they are one part of the larger problem of "invasives" muscling in on native species, hogging resources and decimating land, seas and crops to the tune of over $120 billion a year. Invasives can touch down on American land and waters by various means, ranging from stowing away in ship ballast water to being released into the wild by humans who have cultivated them as ornamental plants or kept them as pets. While non-native species have existed as long as humans have roamed the earth and probably even longer, globalization has accelerated both their spread and the damage they cause.

*Bastard cabbage, a federally designated "noxious weed" commonly seen along roadsides in Texas, has a delicious "earthy, almost parsley-like flavor."*

Like Murphy, many environmental organizations have embraced the idea of promoting the consumption of these invaders—from rogue seaweed to bristly, 200-pound feral hogs—as a way to raise public consciousness and get people involved in combatting a severe threat to biodiversity. "Conservation can get so serious and dire, we want to put a little fun back in," says Laura Huffman, state director of the Texas Nature Conservancy. Most invasives won't be eradicted through human consumption alone, but Huffman and other environmentalists are okay with that. "What's important," she says, "is that we re-popularize and infuse some joy into the conversation over protection of resources." But that begs the question: Do invasives taste good enough to earn a permanent spot on home and restaurant menus?

## Eradication by Mastication

More and more people are trying hard to prove they do. The Corvallis, Oregon-based Institute for Applied Ecology's (IAE) Eradication by Mastication program includes an annual invasive species cook-off and a published cookbook called *The Joy of Cooking Invasives: A Culinary Guide to Biocontrol* (kudzu quiche! nutria eggrolls!). The program will hold a workshop this summer on how to dig, process, and cook up the highly invasive purple varnish clam. Tom Kaye, executive director of IAE, made one of three prize-winning entries at last year's cook-off: battered, deep-fried Cajun bullfrog legs. Second place went to popcorn English house sparrow drumsticks. Despite their poor labor-to-meat ratio, Kaye says, "they were tasty." Third prize went to nutria prepared three ways, including pulled-pork style and made into sausages.

To celebrate Earth Day this year [2013], the Texas Nature Conservancy held a "Malicious but Delicious," dinner, where Austin chefs Ned and Jodi Elliott classed up a bunch of invasives for a four-course menu of popovers with a *salpicon* of tiger prawns, bastard cabbage orecchiette, porchetta of feral hog, and lime and Himalayan blackberry tart. Huffman says there are now 1.5 million feral hogs rototilling the arid Texas soil and eating everything in sight. Producing at least three litters a year for a total of 12 to 13 hoglets, she says, "they're prolific, they're smart, and hard to eradicate because they catch on to our tricks." Diners' response was enthusiastic, reports Elliott, who discovered that bastard cabbage, a federally designated "noxious weed" commonly seen along roadsides in Texas, has a delicious "earthy, almost parsley-like flavor."

## Squirrels and Evil Fish

Conservation biologist Joe Roman runs a website called Eat the Invaders, stocked with informative descriptions of a wide range of invasive species and recipes for preparing them. Roman's personal favorites are green crabs in their soft shell stage sautéed and served with French bread, periwinkle fritters and garlic mustard, which he says "makes an excellent pesto." Lionfish sushi, he adds, is "first-rate."

Roman notes that in England, cooks have targeted the highly invasive gray squirrel, which has become such a popular protein that "they're having a hard time keeping them on the menu." *The Daily Mail* reports that the invading grays have sparked a revival in the Victorian delicacy squirrel pie.

---

*The blue catfish, it turns out, is a far more dangerous invader than the sexier snakehead.*

---

There are signs that Americans, too, are warming to the idea of eating invasives, even outside of specially planned activist events. In the past few years, invasives have been showing up on the menus of restaurants whose primary focus is taste, not environmentalism. Scott Drewno, chef at the top-rated The Source, a Washington, DC, Asian-inflected Wolfgang Puck restaurant, cures snakehead with kaffir lime leaves, lemon grass, cane sugar, ginger and garlic for about nine hours, and then smokes it using *sencha* green tea and serves it with a sauce of garlic chili, soy sauce, rice vinegar and microgreens. Meaty, smoky and exotically spiced, the dish is gaining a following. Although it is not on the lunch menu, "people are coming in and asking for it," Drewno reports.

Chad Wells, chef at Rockfish in Annapolis [Maryland], says of snakehead, "I've done it all: raw, sautéed, grilled, fried, cured, smoked." Two of his menu staples are Asian barbecue-style grilled snakehead tacos and for more adventurous eaters, the snakehead ceviche prepared with orange, mango, peppers and cucumber. Even though snakehead is much pricier than another invasive, blue catfish, Steve Vilnit, director of fisheries marketing for the Maryland Department of Natural Resources, says, "It's almost like a 'Fear Factor' thing, people just want to try it. It looks scary and they want to try this evil fish that can breathe air and 'walk' on land."

## Catfish and Antelope

Often, Rockfish restaurant will get the truly determined "invasivore" who starts with the ceviche then moves on to the tacos, the wild boar sliders and then the blackened Potomac River blue catfish with remoulade, cheddar and grits.

The blue catfish, it turns out, is a far more dangerous invader than the sexier snakehead. "They get so damn big [other fish] can't compete with them," says Wells. They snack on native rockfish, and adult snakeheads have been found in their stomachs. The world record blue catfish: 143 pounds, caught in Virginia waters.

In Ingram, South Texas, Chris Hughes, second-generation owner of Broken Arrow Ranch, has carved out a niche harvesting non-native Nilgai antelope, Axis deer, and feral hogs. The Nilgai, native to India and released in Texas in the 1930s, alone number upwards of 60,000 in Texas, the largest population anywhere in the world. Hughes helps keep populations in check by harvesting them on 30 to 40 Texas ranches a year, taking a mobile processing unit into the field with a U.S. meat inspector in attendance. Customers for the meat include high-end restaurants The French Laundry, Vetri in Philadelphia and celebrity chef John Besh's restaurants in San Antonio.

At Vetri, chef Adam Lionti sears Hughes's antelope rib loin and serves it with an amarone sauce, made with the full-bodied Veneto-region wine of partially dried grapes. "It has a great flavor that goes well with the rich meat; we serve it rare with slices of delicata squash," says chef-owner Marc Vetri. He uses feral hog to enrich a ragu served with chestnut fettuccine. Vetri represents that breed of chef for whom quality and taste trumps any crusading sense of eco-activism. "I'm not using these animals for shock value, or looking at them as 'invasive species'; I don't even know what that means," he says. "Certain meats have interesting tastes and you can pair them up with things that make sense."

*The key with all these dishes is you have to keep it in context for people.*

For others, like Austin butcher Jesse Griffiths, a connection to the land and concern for the environment play a larger role. He serves three different sausages made with either feral hog or invasive venison at his farmer's market butcher shop Dai Due. Among his most popular offerings are Broken Arrow antelope burgers and venison hot dogs, but he also sells plenty of feral hog *cochinita pibil*-style, wrapped in banana leaves and marinated in orange and lime juice. He also does a *carne guisada* stew of venison, tomatoes, onion, garlic and cumin, as well as a gumbo. Griffiths, who authored the book *Afield, A Chef's Guide to Preparing and Cooking Wild Game and Fish*, has completely replaced domestic pork with feral hog on his menu. "People would be unhappy if we went back," he says. The meat is richer and better tasting than the usual varieties, according to many chefs. He also thinks "Texans are especially attuned to the magnitude of the feral hog situation."

At Grapejuice wine bar, located two hours due west of Austin in the town of Kerrville, owner Patrick Wilt uses affordable ground Nilgai antelope for his hugely popular antelope sliders with three different toppings: grilled jalapenos and chipotle-lime aioli; fresh chimichurri sauce and goat cheese; and bacon jam, blue cheese and red onion. Another top-seller is his antelope nachos with beer cheese and chipotle sour cream. Hunting, he says, "is what I do for fun. All we eat at the house is 'invasive species,' as you put it, but I look at everything as lunch or dinner." His approach to selling wild game, he explains, is "make it tasty, fun but still adventurous." Not too adventurous, though. "We used to do a Nilgai carpaccio, which was awesome, but it really scared people," recalls Wilt.

Griffiths, who also offers popular butchering classes that instruct students on every stage of handling feral pigs from shooting to sausage making, agrees: "The key with all these dishes is you have to keep it in context for people. If you tried to sell them wild boar in fermented fig leaves with lingonberry sauce they're going to be like, 'Oh, no.' If you say, 'I made chili,' they understand what it's supposed to taste like."

## Challenging Food

Bun Lai, chef-owner at the New Haven, Connecticut, restaurant Miya Sushi, adopts the opposite approach, doing little to cater to mainstream tastes and expectations. "You can't get nine out of ten of the conventional sushi restaurant dishes here," says Lai, "no shrimp, no farmed salmon, no tuna."

Instead, he offers deep-fried invasive Asian shore crab, each the size of a quarter, served with a sauce made of another invasive, Japanese knotweed; miso soup flavored with a rogue seaweed called dead man's fingers; applewood cold-smoked Asian carp, and spear-caught lionfish sashimi with "a dozen profoundly mouth-numbing spices."

The carp are riddled with pinbones and possess a bone structure that chef Kerry Heffernan says "make an inner-city map of London look uncomplicated." "This stuff isn't meant to be fast food," Lai declares. Miya's challenging fare is not for everyone. "Every single day," he says, "we have people who walk out on us."

In Hawaii, chef and sustainable-food activist Mark Noguchi uses a softer "sell" to interest diners in invasive gorilla seaweed, which smothers coral reefs and chokes native marine life. He blanches then shocks and pickles it, and uses it as a condiment for *poke* (cubed raw tuna in soy dressing). "Old-timers who are familiar with it but have never seen it on a plate before chuckle and think it's kind of cute," he says. It's easy "preaching to the choir" of Whole Foods shoppers, says Noguchi; he wants to reach "the country people who you want to put down the Spam and pick up a salad." So he'll cook up a little batch of something challenging, "slide it out and try to start a dialogue."

---

*Give them a decent price per pound, and fishermen can harvest enough of an invasive species to create "a win-win situation for the environment and people who like eating interesting things."*

---

## Access and Distribution

When it comes to invasive species, palatability is one thing but access and distribution are other, sometime insurmountable barriers to mass consumption. French-born New Orleans chef Philippe Parola, for example, planned to mass-market nutria, the semi-aquatic rodent that is munching its way through coastal Louisiana. It seemed like a winning proposition. Fans say nutria tastes a lot like the rabbit served in European restaurants, and it's such a menace that the state's Nutria Control Program has placed a $4-per-tail bounty on the rodent.

At the height of his nutria promotion campaign, Parola had 20 chefs throughout the state on board, serving the animals as sausages, in gumbo, or slow-cooked in a stew of white wine and vegetables. But a combination of FDA [US Food and Drug Administration] regulations—demanding that the animals be brought to the slaughterhouse alive—and lack of funds sank his plan. Now, Parola is involved in another quest that could hinge on the availability of funds: building a processing plant that turns highly invasive Asian carp into fish cakes and other easy-to-consume products.

In Maryland and Washington D.C., the reason chefs Wells and Drewno are able to put invasive snakehead on their menus is simple: their supplier, a seafood company called ProFish. Two years ago, the company's director of sustainable initiatives, John Rorapaugh, put a bounty on snakehead as incentive for fishermen who were loath to do the work of catching them. The company began offering five dollars a pound for snakehead, far more than the fifty cents a pound they were paid for catfish. Profish sells mostly to "white-tablecloth restaurants getting a pretty penny for their plates," Rorapaugh notes, but they too must sacrifice some profit to promote a fish like snakehead. Through their efforts, Vilnit of the Maryland Department of Natural Resources and Rorapaugh have helped replace farmed catfish with the cheaper and much better-tasting invasive blue catfish, marketing them to school cafeterias, caterers, and hospitals. Last year over 427,000 pounds of the fish was sold by local wholesalers, according to Vilnit. Give them a decent price per pound, and fishermen can harvest enough of an invasive species to create "a win-win situation for the environment and people who like eating interesting things."

For his part, Jackson Landers, author of the book *Eating Aliens*, predicts that in a year we'll be seeing a lot more lionfish on menus. He calls it a fish that "has it all": great-tasting flesh, and a readymade hunting and distribution system. That's because the lionfish share one of their habitats, the coastal waters of the Bahamas, with the spiny lobster, which Landers says "supplies the vast majority of the crustaceans sold at the Red Lobster restaurant chain." A reef fish, lionfish must be caught by hand, either by net or spear. Since lobster traps are illegal, fishermen "are already down there under the water," spearing spiny lobster and "seeing the lionfish," Landers says. Give them a decent price per pound, he suggests, and fishermen could "deny habitat to lionfish over a substantial part of the Caribbean."

## Gourmands and Environmentalists, Together

Avid fisherman and chef Kerry Heffernan, who is writing a cookbook based on his year in Sag Harbor [New York], believes that the best chance of creating an invasive fish commercial harvest is to first create the demand. He sees potential in the blue tilapia, the largest non-native fish species in Florida, and far superior to farmed tilapia because "it's not fed stuff to grow it in six months to harvest." He likes to roast them whole or lightly flour, pan sauté, and finish them with brown butter and thyme.

Some are looking to people like Heffernan to impart the culinary cachet that invasives need to become popular. "It's a chicken and egg situation," says Wenonah Hauter, executive director of Food and Water Watch. "Getting more product available will make it easier for chefs to be able to cook with it. That could be a win-win situation for the environment and people who like eating interesting things." But she adds, "I really think a well-known chef needs to take it up."

Austin Murphy is no famous chef, and doesn't do volume, but he's doing his part. In late June [2013] he staged his third annual Potomac Snakehead Tournament, open to both bow hunters and anglers, drawing 149 contestants who caught over 1,000 pounds of snakehead. Another 500 or so showed up to sample invasive cookery, drink free-flowing Flying Dog beer, listen to live music and ogle snakeheads.

Thanks to all the hunting and fishing he does, Murphy never has to shop for protein at the local grocery store. In addition to fishing, he hunts invasive resident Canada geese, (whose marinated and grilled breasts, he claims, taste "absolutely amazing") and helps cull the local deer population.

Murphy is also enjoying a unique moment in hunter-environmentalist relations: "Even your typical non-hunting, eco-tourist-type person appreciates you trying to remove snakeheads," he says. "They just want to take pictures."

# 4

# Eating Invasives Will Not Reduce Their Impact

*Matt Miller*

*Matt Miller is a writer at the Nature Conservancy.*

*Some conservationists argue that eating invasive species will reduce their numbers and help to eliminate them. However, in many cases, making invasives a food source assimilates them into the culture: hunters don't want to lose the game and consumers don't want to lose the food they enjoy. The truth is invasives are very difficult to get rid of in any case. Rather than trying to eliminate invasives it might be best to accept them as part of the ecology, and enjoy them as food sources when possible.*

Warm spring days evoke a strong memory of my grandmother: She's hunched over the yard, seemingly picking randomly at the grass.

## Eat the Dandelions

Her short stature and rapid movements give the appearance of a dervish. She grips at a plant, plucks and plops it into the bucket, then moves a short distance away to resume her harvest.

My grandmother collected dandelions, a spring bounty she served with a bacon dressing. The bitter greens were not unlike spinach or kale, bitter yet tasty. My grandfather used the flowers to make a potent wine.

This time of year, I so often encounter dandelions shriveled from hefty doses of herbicide. Recalling my grandmother, it seems a waste: Here are delicious, nutritious greens that could be providing some free meals. Instead, they've become toxic reminders of the so-called "war on weeds"—the scorched earth approach to invasive control favored by both surburban lawn owners and conservationists.

Why aren't we instead looking at some non-native, invasive species as a sustainable source for fresh food, local food?

The idea is popular. Books like Jackson Landers' upcoming *Eating Aliens* encourage local foodies to eat such invasives as iguanas and nutrias. Marine conservationists have launched campaigns to encourage restaurants to carry lionfish, a species devastating coral reefs.

Even governments have urged their citizens to eat non-native gray squirrels (in Britain) and camels (in Australia).

---

*Encouraging people to eat invasives may have unintended consequences. There's a real risk ... that people will start actually* liking *said invasives.*

---

As history shows, people can certainly eat their way through populations of species. As such, eating invasives doesn't only provide good food, it's good conservation.

Or is it?

## Good Food, Not Good Ecology

An upcoming paper by ecologist Martin Nunez and others to be published in *Conservation Letters*, the journal of the Society of Conservation Biology, encourages skepticism to this approach.

In the paper, they argue that encouraging people to eat invasives may have unintended consequences. There's a real risk, the authors argue, that people will start actually *liking* said invasives.

Entrepreneurs could develop markets for them; hunters could enjoy pursuing them. Invasives could become a part of the local culture.

As a review in *Conservation* magazine points out, native Hawaiians often oppose eradication measures for non-native pigs because pig hunting and eating is so clearly linked to their culture.

I can relate: On a recent weekend, my friends and organic gardeners Clay and Josie Erskine asked me to their farm to hunt the non-native (in Idaho) wild turkeys that had begun raiding their gardens.

As we looked across their farm, ring-necked pheasants ran from the kale patch. Valley quail called from literally every corner of the property.

"Every one of them is a non-native species," Josie sighed. "And they're all absolutely devastating to vegetable farmers like us."

Non-native quail, pheasants and turkeys have a constituency, though. Membership organizations advocate for their conservation. Landowners can receive government funding for practices that largely benefit these birds.

I reluctantly admit, as a non-native gamebird hunter, I would oppose any effort to eliminate these species.

Could campaigns to eat kudzu or camels or carp actually have the reverse effect? Could such campaigns lead to people protecting or spreading them?

It bears serious thought.

The risks need to be recognized. So, too, do the benefits.

Intensive invasive species control poses risks of its own. With its war metaphors and scorched earth campaigns, invasives eradication often requires hefty doses of toxic chemicals. And just as often, weeds or invasive animals still flourish. Aside from cases on small islands such as Santa Cruz, complete eradication is usually impossible.

Recognizing dandelions as a food source will not eradicate the plant. But spraying dandelions doesn't, either.

In many ways, eating invasives is not a control measure so much as it is a new way of interacting with non-native species. Through eating them, they become part of our environment rather than "enemies." And because they're prolific and abundant, they make ideal sustainable, low-carbon, local food sources.

Despite our best efforts, invasive species already thrive in our midst. Is serving them for dinner really going to make them even more prevalent?

Doubtful. These species are here to stay. It's time to recognize them as a truly sustainable and abundant food source. I'll take the fried iguana served over a bed of dandelion greens, please.

# 5

# Invasive Species Threaten Global Biodiversity

*Roser Toll*

*Roser Toll is a correspondent for the AFP (Agence France-Presse) news service.*

*Invasive species can destroy biodiversity, pushing out native creatures and altering ecological habitats. This problem can be compounded by global warming, which may weaken native species, giving invaders a chance to take over. And of course the most dangerous invasive species of all is humans, who can cause great ecological damage when they move into a new area.*

Until a few decades ago, there were no beavers in Patagonia. That changed when 20 pairs of the tree-chewing creature were introduced with the hopes of creating a fur industry.

## Species Moving Farther, Faster

Today, their numbers have exploded and they pose a serious threat to the South American area's biodiversity.

Species have always moved. The wind carries seeds; animals swim and fly. But not all are capable of crossing the Atlantic or the Andes.

In ways planned or unforeseen, humans have introduced species, and the newcomers quickly become invaders and threaten to destroy the native flora and fauna of their adopted homes.

"When we lose biodiversity, we are losing a bank of genetic material" that we need for food or to create medicines, said Fernando Baeriswyl, a project coordinator for the Global Environment Fund specializing in invasive species in Chile.

In North America and Europe, beavers live in balance with their natural habitat. But in Patagonia, the native trees don't regenerate fast enough to keep pace with the animals' rampant destructive powers. Plus beavers in Patagonia don't have any natural predators, like bears or wolves.

With the trees they fell, beavers build dams up to three meters tall. These structures can change waterways and lead to flooding or drying of traditional river ways.

Within a few years of their export to the southern tip of Patagonia, the animals had expanded their range around the region.

Their advance has been so swift that today they represent a menace that is proving hard to control. Authorities in Argentina and Chile have authorized the hunting of the animals, but these efforts have not stopped the beaver.

---

*Invasive species travel in ships, in clothes and shoes, or even in people's stomachs.*

---

Chile and Argentina are now determined to completely eradicate the tree-chewers, said Adrian Schiavini, a beaver specialist from a regional research center.

## Invasive Blackberries

In the Huilo Huilo reserve in southern Chile, dozens of invasive-species experts got together last month [October 2014] for the country's first national meeting focused on invasive species in protected areas, to try to address the lack of knowledge and rules to tackle the problem.

Invasive species travel in ships, in clothes and shoes, or even in people's stomachs. When they get to a new environment, they can often proliferate thanks to a lack of natural predators.

As they spread, they can gradually alter entire ecosystems, transforming the natural diets of local species or themselves being eaten by other animals. In the worst cases, they can wipe out entire native species.

According to specialists, along with pollution and climate change, invasive species are one of the most damaging challenges for our planet.

"Climate change is causing a major vulnerability for certain species to the effects of invasive species," said Victor Carrion, the administrator of the Galapagos National Park in Ecuador.

The University of Chile carried out a study showing that the Andean country has 119 exotic invasive species, 27 of which are threatening biodiversity, including the European wasp, an invasive slime called "rock snot," red deer and wild boar, among others.

The same can happen with flowers. If we find a flower we like and take it home to plant in the garden, the results can lead to an ecological disaster.

That's what happened with blackberry bushes.

"When that arrives, it's a death sentence," Baeriswyl said.

The shrub invades the ground under trees and stops other plants from photosynthesizing, as well as slurping up their water.

Even rabbits, dogs and goats can cause problems. Many people think they are native to the region, but they would never have reached many places without human intervention.

## Death to the Invaders?

When Europeans first started sailing to South America, they left goats on islands to ensure they had food for future voyages. The animals devoured many plants, causing erosion and altering ecosystems.

Centuries later, in the Galapagos Islands, more than 270,000 goats were eliminated on 10 islands, along with cats, pigeons, donkeys and rodents, Carrion said.

Animal advocates have criticized these approaches.

In the case of beavers, the animals will be caught in traps that ensure a quick death.

But the world's most invasive species, of course, is us. People quickly spread across the globe from Africa, altering ecosystems and impacting endemic species as they went.

# 6

# Pushed by Climate Change, Fish Invasion of Arctic Bodes Well for Fishermen

*Brittany Patterson*

*Brittany Patterson is a reporter for E&E Publishing.*

*Climate change is allowing southern fish species to move into the warming Arctic. Experts think that the result will be a rich mix of species, rather than extinction of natives, since most of the fish moving north are not predators. The result could be improvement in fishing and increased biodiversity in many parts of the Arctic. The new ecology may be difficult to manage and is hard to predict, but it need not be a disaster for native species.*

More than 3 million years ago, the Arctic became a fish highway as species from the north Pacific Ocean spread through the Bering Strait and into the Arctic Ocean and then into the north Atlantic Ocean.

Now it's beginning to happen again.

A new study published in the journal *Nature Climate Change* suggests that as climate change warms the Arctic over the next century, the natural ice barrier that has kept these two marine biotas separate will disappear, allowing fish from the Atlantic and Pacific to mix. This will create unknown consequences for fishing communities from Norway to Alaska, as well as the ecology of both regions.

Using predictive modeling, a group of international scientists across multiple fields showed that once ice melts and the interchange begins, changing oceanographic conditions like sea temperatures, salinity and currents will contribute to changes in the distribution of many commercial fish. Biodiversity is likely to explode in places like the Svalbard coast, the Barents Sea, the coasts of Iceland and the Alaskan coast.

"Our results show that the North Atlantic and North Pacific, which contribute nearly 40 percent to global commercial fish landings, are likely to be ecologically affected by new arrivals of species with climate change," Mary Wisz, co-leader of the study and a senior ecosystem scientist at DHI, a private consultancy and research institute based in Denmark, said in an email.

"Our models forecast there will be an explosion of fish biodiversity in these areas during this century."

Researchers have long suggested a mixing like this would occur in the Arctic, but new availability of data on where fish species are found, as well as models that forecast future conditions, enabled the multidisciplinary team to predict the forthcoming geographical distributions for 515 of the most common species found in the northern latitudes.

---

*This interspecies mixing [in the Arctic] will probably impact diversity more positively and increase productivity.*

---

"We can see the extent of sea ice shrinking, and it looks like projections we have of an open Arctic passage are going to come true and sooner than we thought," said Jason Link, a senior scientist for ecosystem management with the National Oceanic and Atmospheric Administration who was not involved in the study. "What we can say is there will be change. What is more difficult is the direction of that change."

## A Recent Precedent

In November of 1869, the Suez Canal, a man-made waterway through Egypt, connected the Mediterranean and Red seas. It provided scientists with a modern example of what happens when two formerly separate marine biotas mix.

The Red Sea is generally saltier and contains less nutrients than the Atlantic, so the Red Sea species have advantages over Atlantic species in the eastern Mediterranean Sea. About 300 invasive species have been cataloged in the Mediterranean and pose significant ecological challenges for native species.

"In the Mediterranean, when we opened the Suez Canal, we turned over the food web from species coming in," Link said.

In the Arctic, however, Link said he expects the impacts from this interspecies mixing will probably impact diversity more positively and increase productivity.

Nearly 40 percent of the world's commercial fishing landings are in the Arctic, and that will create a huge economic opportunity for fisheries.

Already climate change has pushed mackerel northward toward eastern Greenland, contributing to a 53,000-ton catch in 2013, Wisz said.

As resources in the Arctic are being unfrozen by climate change, from oil to gas and a potential growth in fishing capacity, one concern is how to manage the area with the interests that will want to exploit them.

The expansive geography and international nature of the Arctic will make managing the area an interesting challenge, Link added.

"That's a lot of fish," Wisz said in an email. "The challenges of course will be that we don't know how things will play out in these new ecological contexts."

## A Fish-Rich Mixing Bowl

For example, the researchers' models indicated that few top predators are expected to be involved in the coming mixing, with the exception of Atlantic cod and lingcod, two aggressive predators that have the potential to dominate their new ecosystems.

"If cod moves to Pacific Northwest, there are already species like that there," Link said. "How they will interact is unknown, but it looks like there could be competition with those who eat the same types of food."

On a positive note, Geerat Vermeij, a distinguished professor of Earth and planetary sciences at the University of California, Davis, who has written on this subject before, said although the coming invasion will certainly have effects, he doesn't think species extinctions will be one of them.

Vermeij expects to see the diversity of Atlantic fauna grow in parallel to what happened millions of years ago, as he put it, "in the recent geological past."

For example, every common fish found today on the New England coast originated in the Pacific, he said.

Wisz said her team would next like to use emerging dynamic modeling tools to look at how fish species are expected to disperse based on current patterns and spawning requirements as well as examine how food webs might change. This type of data could help fisheries prepare for the coming changes and inform shipping routes to bypass areas that might become fish-rich.

Link said it's important to note that in addition to warming, there are other changes driven by climate change that will affect the Arctic such as ocean acidification and shifts in global circulation, which were not factored into the new research.

As far as what humans can do to prevent or prepare for the coming invasion, Vermeij said it's a matter of when, not if.

"It's just a prediction, so they can go wrong," Vermeij said, "but this is one place where knowledge of the geological record really can inform us of the potential in the future. Humans certainly can't prevent it or really prepare for it, but it would be nice to document it."

# 7

# Bio-Control Is Environmentally Dangerous

### Death of a Million Trees

*Death of a Million Trees is a blog dedicated to the preservation of all trees in the San Francisco Bay area.*

*California is trying to eradicate non-native cheatgrass with a deadly fungus. This is meant to be safe bio-control. However, bio-control can go amiss, escape the lab before proper testing, and cause unforeseen environmental damage. In addition, there is no certainty of what will replace the cheatgrass if it is all eradicated. Cheatgrass seems to have gained a foothold in part because of global warming; eliminating the grass will not deal with the underlying problem. As a result, bio-control is unreliable and dangerous as a way to attack invasive species.*

We were recently reminded of the use of biological controls to eradicate non-native species when we learned that Australian insects may have been illegally imported to California to kill eucalyptus which had been virtually pest free until 1983. So, an article in the New York Times about the development of a fungus for the purpose of killing cheatgrass (*Bromus tectorum*) caught our attention. The fungus has been given the ominous name, Black Fingers of Death, for the black stubs of cheatgrass infected with the fungus.

Cheatgrass is one of the non-native grasses that have essentially replaced native grasses throughout the United States.

It was probably introduced with ship ballast and wheat seed stock in about 1850. As we have reported, native grasses were quickly replaced by the non-native grasses which tolerate the heavy grazing of domesticated animals brought by settlers. Native Americans had no domesticated animals.

Biological controls have frequently caused more serious damage than the problems they were intended to solve. Therefore, we would hope that their intended target is doing more damage than the potential damage of its biological control. We must ask if the cure is worse than the disease. And in this case, we don't think the damage done by cheatgrass justifies inflicting it with the Black Fingers of Death.

## The Track Record of Biological Control

Biological control is the intentional introduction of animals, pests, microbes, fungi, pathogens, etc., for the purpose of killing a plant or animal which is perceived to be causing a problem. The ways in which some of these biocontrols have gone badly wrong are as varied and as many as the methods used.

Introduced species of plants are said to have an initial advantage in their new home because their pests and competitors are not always introduced with them. This is the "enemy release hypothesis" popular amongst native plant advocates to explain the tendency of non-native plants to be invasive. However, this is usually a temporary advantage which is exaggerated by native plant advocates who do not seem to recognize the speed with which native species can adapt to new species, and *vice versa*.

Therefore, a popular method of biological control is to import the predator or competitor of the non-native species which is considered invasive. This is only effective if the pest is selective in its host. There are many examples of such introductions which did not prove to be selective: "For the United States mainland, Hawaii, and the Caribbean region, [R.W.] Pemberton (2000) listed 15 species of herbivorous biocontrol insects that have extended their feeding habits to 41 species of native plants. . . ." Although most of the unintended hosts were related to the intended hosts, some were not.

---

*Nature has foiled the best efforts of the scientists designing biological controls for non-native species of plants and animals.*

---

Similar shifts from target to nontarget species have occurred for biocontrol agents of animal pests: "For parasitoids introduced to North America for control of insect pests, [Bradford A.] Hawkins and [Paul C.] Marino (1997) found that 51 (16.7%) of the 313 introduced species were recorded from nontarget hosts. For Hawaii, 37 (32.3%) of 115 parasitoid species were noted to use nontarget hosts . . . biological control introductions are considered to be responsible for extinctions of at least 15 native moth species [in Hawaii]."

There are also several cases of biological controls escaping from the laboratory setting before they had been adequately tested and approved for release. A virus escaped the laboratory in Australia and killed 90% of the rabbits in its initial spread through the wild population. Very quickly, the virus evolved to a less fatal strain that killed less than 50% of the rabbits it infected. A second virus was then tested and also escaped its laboratory trial and has spread through the rabbit population throughout Australia.

A fly being considered for introduction to control yellow starthistle apparently escaped and damaged a major cash crop of safflower in California according to a study published in 2001, illustrating the risks of biocontrols to agriculture.

This is but a brief description of the diverse ways in which nature has foiled the best efforts of the scientists designing biological controls for non-native species of plants and animals. The source of this information therefore concludes, ". . . many releases of species have inadequate justification . . .

The first goal of research must be to show that the introduced biological control agent will not itself cause damage." Given this wise advice, we will return to the question, "What damage is being done by cheatgrass and does that damage justify the introduction of The Black Fingers of Death?"

## Why Is Cheatgrass Considered a Problem?

Cheatgrass is one of the many non-native annual grasses which have replaced the native grasses which were not adapted to the grazing of domesticated animals. Cheatgrass is a valuable nutritional source for grazing animals when it is green and loses much of its nutritional value when it dries.

---

*One of the causes of the expanding range of cheatgrass is increasing levels of the greenhouse gases contributing to climate change.*

---

Grazing is only one of the types of disturbance which create opportunities for non-native grasses to expand their range into unoccupied ground. Fire is another disturbance which gives cheatgrass a competitive advantage over native grasses because it uses available moisture and germinates before native grasses can gain a foothold on the bare ground cleared by fire.

Cheatgrass is said to increase fire frequency by increasing fuel load and continuity. Unfortunately, increasing levels of $CO_2$ (carbon dioxide) in the atmosphere is increasing the fuel load of cheatgrass: ". . . the indigestible portion of above-ground plant material [of cheatgrass] . . . increased with increasing $CO_2$."

Carbon dioxide is the predominant greenhouse gas which is contributing to climate change. And increasing frequency of wildfires is one of the consequences of the higher temperatures associated with climate change. Therefore, one of the causes of the expanding range of cheatgrass is increasing levels of the greenhouse gases contributing to climate change. Rather than address the underlying cause, we are apparently planning to poison the cheatgrass with a deadly fungus.

If we are successful in killing the cheatgrass, what will occupy the bare ground? Will native grasses and shrubs return? Will whatever occupies the bare ground be an improvement over the cheatgrass which has some nutritional value to grazing animals? The US Forest Service plant database gives us this warning, "Care must be taken with methods employed to control cheatgrass so that any void left by cheatgrass removal is not filled with another nonnative invasive species that may be even less desirable."

## Recapitulating Familiar Themes

The project to develop a deadly fungus to kill cheatgrass is another example of the issues that we often discuss on [Death of a] Million Trees [blog]:

> Are the risks of the methods used to eradicate non-native species being adequately assessed and evaluated before projects are undertaken?

> Are the underlying conditions—such as climate change—that have contributed to an "invasion" being addressed by the methods used to eradicate them? If not, will the effort be successful?

> Is the damage done by the "invasion" greater than the damage done by the methods used to eradicate the invader? Is the cure worse than the disease?

We do not believe that these questions are being addressed by the many "restoration" projects we see in the San Francisco Bay Area. Consequently, we believe that these projects often do more harm than good.

# 8

# Most Dangerous Invasive Species Include Pigs, Mussels, and Bees

*Faine Greenwood*

*Faine Greenwood is a reporter at the* GlobalPost.

*Invasive species destroy native wildlife and cause economic and ecological damage. Some of the worst invasive species include Burmese pythons, which eat native species in Florida; zebra mussels, which clog waterways in many parts of the United States; and rabbits, which ran wild after their introduction in Australia. More needs to be done to eradicate invasive species and to prevent species from crossing waterways and borders and becoming invasives.*

Invasive species are among us, and they're likely here to stay. These invaders from foreign lands alight on new soil and decide they'd like to set up housekeeping, often wreaking havoc on the local ecosystem, and costing millions in property and habitat destruction to beleaguered human bystanders.

"When people move either by accident or on purpose certain plants, animals, or microorganisms to places where they are not part of nature they invade and cause great harm," Chris Dionigi, deputy director of the National Invasive Species Council, told *GlobalPost*.

Here's some of the most loathsome offenders.

## Pythons and Mussels

### 1. Burmese pythons

The massive Burmese python is perhaps the most menacing invasive species in America, as one might expect from a gigantic, aggressive Southeast Asian snake. It's not entirely clear how these beasts first made it to Florida—zoo escapees from hurricanes and lousy pet owners are likely culprits—but the reptiles soon realized that the balmy, marshy conditions in the Everglades were close to their homeland.

Capable of consuming smallish alligators, wild boar, and other seemingly unlikely prey, these tenacious creatures can get massive. Earlier this month [August 2012], a 17-foot long, 165-pound female was caught in the Florida Everglades—and she was carrying 84 eggs.

Even though Burmese pythons are currently restricted to Florida, climate change could mean these giant snakes could show up in more northern climates in the near future, according to *USA Today*.

Although wild pythons have yet to kill anybody insofar as I can determine, pet Burmese pythons have been known to occasionally strangle small children and pets. (Parents: for God's sake, get a Beagle.)

Curiously enough, it's still extremely easy for Americans to purchase pet Burmese Pythons on the Internet, for a mere $299.99. They're not offered on Amazon.com yet, but stay tuned!

---

*It's currently estimated that there's around 700,000 mussels per square meter in the hardest hit bits of the Great Lakes.*

---

There is a hunting season in Florida on Burmese pythons, in case you want to mount a *real* conversation starter above your living room couch.

2. Zebra mussels

These aren't the benevolent kind of mussels you cook in white wine with some garlic and fennel. These menacing bivalves have clogged up waterways, destroyed boats, and generally made life miserable on the water for wide swaths of the USA.

The mussels are native to the inland Eastern European Caspian sea, according to this handy King County, Washington website [www.kingcounty.gov], and only arrived here around 1988, likely clinging to the hulls of European ships undetected. The little jerks soon gummed up the Great Lakes with dizzying speed, and it's currently estimated that there's around 700,000 mussels per square meter in the hardest hit bits of the Great Lakes.

The mussels ruin ecosystems because they filter out nearly all the nutrient-rich plankton in the waters they infest, starving other creatures that rely on these nutrients, according to the Gulf of Maine Research Institute [GMR].

Zebra mussels damage property: the GMR says the mussels can clog "water-intake pipes and screens of drinking water facilities, industrial facilities, power generating plants, golf course irrigation pipes, cooling systems of boat engines, and boat hulls."

That also includes your fancy multi-million dollar yacht. *Zebra mussel don't care.*

And no, we can't eat them. Zebra mussels don't get very big, for one thing—and as filter feeders, they soak up all the unpleasant gunk in the water. Further, according to Buffalo Rising Online, zebra mussels store botulism toxins in their bodies, causing great harm to the animals that do eat them. Yummy!

## Rabbits and Bees

3. Rabbits

Bunny rabbits may be fluffy and adorable, but they're an absolute scourge in Australia, where the hopping creatures have done a remarkably thorough job of eradicating native wildlife. European rabbits obviously aren't much of a menace individually, but their remarkable powers of reproducing— and eating—mean that they can decimate farms and destroy ecosystems with shocking speed.

A mere 24 rabbits introduced into Australia in 1859 as a hunting diversion for European settlers quickly ballooned into 10 billion hopping menaces by the 1920s, according to the Foundation for Rabbit Free Australia. The animals devastated farmers' crops and destroyed the land's carrying capacity, according to this University of Texas report. A massive "rabbit proof fence" erected in Western Australia to stop the bunny plague didn't help much.

---

*Killer bees, known to scientists as Africanized honey bees, are crossbreeds between our beloved, fuzzy European worker bees and way more hardcore African bees.*

---

Rabbits are believed to be responsible for the extinction of a number of small marsupials in the same ecological niche in Australia, and although human-introduced disease have made a dent in their numbers, they continue to threaten native plants and animals. . . .

4. Killer bees (Africanized Honey Bees)

Remember when the US *lost its collective mind* over an impending invasion of enraged Africanized honey-bees? I do (as well as the crappy horror movies the mania spawned, unfortunately).

Killer bees, known to scientists as Africanized honey bees, are crossbreeds between our beloved, fuzzy European worker bees and way more hardcore African bees.

According to the Smithsonian [Institution], Brazilian scientists decided to crossbreed the varieties to improve honey production, but found the resulting crossbred bees had a nasty temperament, and attacked with much more ferocity than the European bees. And then they escaped. And headed North.

Among the differences, according to the USDA [US Department of Agriculture], Africanized honey bees "swarm" (move house en masse) more often than the milder European variety—and they also will fiercely protect a much larger "home" than their relatives.

The bees first hit the US in 1990, according to the Smithsonian, and have been here ever since.

Killer bee mania has faded somewhat in the US since the 1990s, but they still do kill people: in 2010, a 73-year-old man was killed by the insects when he accidentally disturbed their nest with a bulldozer. . . .

## Boar, and the Worst Invasive Ever

5. European Wild Boar

Huge, fast, aggressive and *delicious* when braised: that's the feral hog, a distant relative of the pinkish Wilburs you may be more familiar with. According to PBS [Public Broadcasting Service], these massive beasts were introduced in Florida all the way back in 1539 from their native Eurasian territory by bacon-loving Spanish explorers, and they've been tearing up forests and terrorizing humans ever since.

Boar destroy ecosystems by rooting up native plants and eating food other animals rely on. They're also a pain for farmers, eating sugar cane, corn, and other cashcrops and not responding very nicely to attempts to get them to leave. Mississippi State guesses that wild pigs cause around $1.5 billion in environmental and agriculture damage *annually*.

On the bright side? Unlike zebra mussels, the oft-hunted (if hard to kill) wild boar tastes delicious. Here, have some recipes! This is one of the few invasive species where eating a delicious roast can be considered a positive step towards conservation.

Here's a video [on youtube.com] of what appears to be a Burmese python post snacking on a wild boar. Never say I did nothing for you. (There's also this harrowing footage [on youtube.com] of an incredibly dangerous wild boar approaching a daring camera person, but don't say I didn't warn you.)

Is there a single *worst* invasive species? Not really—they're all pretty bad, says Dionigi, the deputy director of the National Invasive Species Council.

Invasive species "degrade, consume, and displace our crops, farms, gardens, and favorite places," he told *GlobalPost*. "No area, no matter how cherished, is free from the threat." (Including your own backyard, *natch*.)

"Because of these complex impacts, some of which are only now being understood, it is difficult to identify a single species as the 'worst,'" added Dionigi. "However, invasive species are a leading cause of a loss of animal and plant species world-wide."

Invasive species also can be really expensive, added Dionigi—and not just for the federal government.

"The federal government alone spends over $1.5 billion on invasive species prevention and control each year," he said. "However, the bulk of the costs of controlling invasive species fall to states, tribes, local governments, and private land owners." Think about this if you ever decide your child's irritating exotic pet might just be better off in the wild.

9

# Wild Horse Population in the United States Is Invasive and Disruptive

*National Horse and Burro Rangeland Management Coalition*

*The National Horse and Burro Rangeland Management Coalition is a partnership of wildlife conservation and sportsmen organizations that works toward effective management of wild horse and burro populations.*

*Wild horses were native to the Americas thousands of years ago; however, those herds died out, and current horse populations introduced to the United States are invasive. Horse and burro populations are currently too high and threaten native species and ecosystems. Horse and burro populations therefore need to be controlled and limited to protect grazing land and native species.*

M<sup>yth</sup>

Equids evolved in the United States; therefore the current populations of horses in the United States are native.

Fact

The horses seen in the American West today are descended from a domesticated breed introduced from Europe, and are therefore a non-native species and not indigenous.

Although many horse lineages evolved in North America, they went extinct approximately 11,400 years ago during the Pleistocene era. All horses (*Equus caballus*) and burros (*E. asinus*) now present in North America are descendants of those domesticated in Eurasia and Africa and thus subjected to many generations of selective breeding before they were introduced to North America by settlers.

Exotic, non-native species are among the most widespread and serious threats to the integrity of native wildlife populations because they invade and can degrade native ecosystems. When invasive species are perceived as a natural component of the environment, the damages they inflict on native systems are overlooked. As a result, some groups advocate conservation and management of exotic species that promote their continued presence in landscapes where they are not native, leading to the decline of native species.

---

*Areas inhabited by horses and burros tend to have fewer plant species, less vegetative cover, and an increased susceptibility to invasive plant species.*

---

The horses and burros that roam freely across areas of western North America and along parts of the Atlantic coast are examples of such species: they are iconic and beloved by some, but damage crucial wildlife habitat and require improved and sustainable management practices. The numbers and impact of these horses and burros can be difficult to control, amplifying their effects on native habitat and wildlife. In some cases, current management of horses and burros and their effects diverts resources (human and financial) from management of native species and habitat.

## Horses and Environmental Damage

Myth

Horse and burro populations on Bureau of Land Management [BLM] lands have not reached environmentally damaging levels.

Fact

Horse and burro populations have surpassed the Appropriate Management Levels (AMLs) set by the Bureau of Land Management and their scientific team, and are damaging native plant and animal species.

With federal protection provided by the Wild Free-Roaming Horse and Burro Act of 1971, numbers of horses on public lands rose from approximately 17,300 in 1971 to an estimated peak of 57,200 in 1978. As of February 2013, the Bureau of Land Management estimated that 40,605—33,780 horses and 6,825 burros—are roaming BLM-managed rangelands in 10 Western states. That number is nearly 14,000 more than the West-wide Appropriate Management Level of 26,667. AML's, determined through an in-depth environmental analysis and decision process that includes public involvement, are set to ensure healthy rangelands that can support wildlife, permitted livestock, and wild horses and burros.

The BLM monitors horse and burro population numbers and rangeland conditions. If the AML is exceeded for a herd management area, BLM calculates how many animals need to be removed from public rangelands to improve the health of the land.

According to results from the Clan Alpine Mountains, differences in vegetation and small mammal activity can be observed between horse-excluded and horse-occupied areas when population numbers exceed established AMLs by less than 10 percent in the occupied areas. Areas inhabited by horses tend to have fewer plant species, less shrub cover, lower occurrence of native grasses, and more invasive plants. Many small reptiles and mammals that depend on burrows and brush cover to survive and breed are less abundant in horse-occupied sites. In particular, species that have specific habitat requirements are more at risk, while animals that thrive in disturbed landscapes, such as deer mice, become more common in areas occupied by horses.

## Horses Threaten Ecosystems

Myth

Horses and burros cannot alter ecosystems.

Fact

Horse and burro populations that exceed Appropriate Management Levels are a distinct and serious threat to ecosystem health.

Horses and burros damage landscapes by trampling vegetation, hardpacking the soil, and over-grazing forage plants. Horse grazing also leads to indirect damage by reducing the amount of precipitation that can penetrate the soil, increasing erosion, and increasing soil temperatures which leads to a shift in plant and animal communities. Areas inhabited by horses and burros tend to have fewer plant species, less vegetative cover, and an increased susceptibility to invasive plant species, which can have ecosystem-wide implications.

Small reptiles and mammals in western North America that depend on burrows and brush cover to survive and breed are less diverse and less abundant in horse- and burro-occupied sites. These reptiles and mammals are an important component of rangeland systems, serving as a link in the food web and performing numerous critical ecosystem functions. The diet of horses and burros overlaps a great deal with that of bighorn sheep, and uncontrolled horse and burro populations have been predicted to lead to greater competition for forage and a decline in the populations of bighorn sheep and other native animals. Ecosystem-wide effects are of particular concern for sagebrush dependent species, including the Greater Sage-Grouse, which is a candidate for listing under the Endangered Species Act.

Horses have a greater impact on rangeland vegetation than other ungulates [hoofed mammals] because of their anatomy and foraging habits. Horses can consume 1.25 times the amount of forage than a cow of equivalent mass. Horses have both upper and lower front incisors and flexible lips, allowing them to crop vegetation closer to the ground than other ungulates. Horses also have hooves designed with one round toe, unlike other ungulates on the range, allowing them to paw vegetation out by the roots, killing the entire plant. All of these physical characteristics can delay the recovery of vegetation.

## Horses Are Not in Danger

Myth

The Bureau of Land Management is sending horses to slaughter to decrease their population.

Fact

The Bureau of Land Management does not and has not sold or sent horses or burros to slaughter.

Under the Wild Horses and Burros Act, euthanasia is identified as an appropriate management tool to reduce numbers of unadoptable horses. However, the Bureau of Land Management currently uses alternative options to euthanasia. Excess horses that aren't adopted by the public are held in temporary or permanent enclosures.

In an effort to ensure the humane treatment of horses and burros gathered from public rangelands and to increase public transparency of gatherings, the Bureau of Land Management announced four internal policy updates in 2013 to its National Wild Horse and Burro Program. One update limits the number of animals sold to an individual, group, or holding location over a six month period and specifies trailer requirements in an effort to prevent the sale of wild horses and burros to slaughter.

Myth

The Bureau of Land Management's policies are driving horses to extinction.

Fact

The Bureau of Land Management ensures horse and burro population numbers do not drop below the sustainable level to maintain viable populations.

The Bureau of Land Management is attempting to reach the appropriate management level of 26,500 horses and burros on Western public rangelands, which is 14,000 animals less than the current Western population. The transfer of horses from the range to temporary or permanent enclosures is used to manage for a sustainable level that would decrease the negative consequences for horse health, native forage and fauna, and other multiple uses. BLM closely monitors herd population levels and genetics to ensure the population does not decrease below a sustainable level.

## Controls Are Needed

Myth

Horse populations will stabilize in a healthy and natural way if left alone.

Fact

There is no scientific evidence to support the idea that horses can limit their own population naturally.

Since the native species of North American horses went extinct in the Pleistocene era, the western United States has become more arid and many of the horses' natural predators, such as the American lion and saber-toothed cat, have also gone extinct, substantially changing the ecosystem and ecological roles horses and burros play.

Because these animals do not have natural predators and their populations are capable of doubling every four years without management, horse populations can increase to a point where food will become limited, leading to starvation. This population crash would likely happen after the range ecosystem has been damaged beyond repair, after which noxious and/or exotic weeds could be expected to replace native grasses and forbs. This would negatively affect water, air, and soil quality, further impacting entire ecosystems, including humans and wildlife.

Myth

Horse populations typically increase by less than 10 percent every year.

Fact

The Bureau of Land Management's recent population statistics as well as multiple peer-reviewed studies have shown that horse herds increase by approximately 20 percent every year.

---

*The Bureau of Land Management removes horses and burros from public rangelands to ensure rangeland health.*

---

Horse populations often grow at rates of 18–25 percent per year, which means these populations have the ability to double in four years. Growth rate is dependent on three factors: fecundity, mortality, and survival. The high population growth rate of these horses is due to their high reproductive rate, the lack of natural predators to keep their populations in check, and the increased survival rate due to artificial aids such as manmade water supplies.

Myth

The Bureau of Land Management removes horses to make room for more cattle grazing on public rangelands.

Fact

The Bureau of Land Management removes horses and burros from public rangelands to ensure rangeland health.

Removal of excess horses and burros by the Bureau of Land Management from overpopulated areas is in accordance with multiple land-use mandates and protects natural resources and rangeland health. The effect of rangeland degradation is of particular concern for declining big horned sheep and sagebrush dependent species, including the Greater Sage-Grouse, which is a candidate for listing under the Endangered Species Act.

Authorized livestock grazing on BLM-managed land has declined by nearly 50 percent since the 1940's, and has declined on public rangelands by 30 percent since 1971—from 12.1 million AUMs [Animal unit month: the amount of forage needed by an animal unit (AU) grazing for one month] to 8.3 million AUMs in 2011. Meanwhile, the horse and burro population has increased from an estimated 17,300 to 25,000 in 1971 to a minimum of 37,000 on the range in 2012.

Myth

Horse gathers, especially those using helicopters, are harmful to the horses and should be prevented.

Fact

Roundups of horses do not affect behavior or reproduction of horses and are necessary to humanely maintain healthy, sustainable populations on rangelands.

The American Association of Equine Practitioners (AAEP) determined that the Bureau of Land Management horse gather practices are humane, efficient, and effective, and that after gathers, horses are in good condition and do not display signs of distress. The level of exhaustion following a gather observed by the AAEP task force was noted to be equivalent to the level of exhaustion exhibited by a domestic horse post workout or competition. No severe injuries requiring veterinary care were observed by the AAEP task force during gathers and only 5% of horses experienced superficial abrasions. Section 1338 of the 1971 Wild Free-Roaming Horse and Burro Act authorizes BLM's use of helicopters and motorized vehicles in its management of horses and burros. Studies have shown that horse gathers via helicopter have no deleterious impact on horse foraging, social behavior, or foaling success. Gathers are a necessary management practice as horse populations become unsustainable.

Myth

Two million wild horses roamed the United States in the late 1800s through early 1900s.

Fact

This number, used by many advocacy groups, was taken out of context and has never been and cannot be substantiated.

The source of this number, used by many advocacy groups, is the book titled *The Mustangs* (1952) by J. Frank Dobie. This folklore author noted that no scientific estimates of wild horse numbers were made in the 19th century or early 20th century. His misunderstood quote is as follows: "All guessed numbers are mournful to history. My own guess is that at no time were there more than a million mustangs in Texas and no more than a million others scattered over the remainder of the West." Mr. Dobie's admitted guess of no more than two million mustangs has over the years been transformed by many into an asserted "fact" that two million mustangs actually roamed America in the late 1800s/early 1900s.

Regardless what the herd count may have been at the turn of the 20th century, more relevant are the questions of what Congress intended in passing the Wild Horse and Burro Act in 1971, and how many head the range can actually accommodate. Congress directed the Bureau of Land Management to manage horses within the areas they inhabited at the time of the Act's passage (herd areas). It also directed the agency to do so in a scientifically sound manner that allowed for the continued multiple-use of herd areas. Accordingly, the BLM established scientifically-derived appropriate management levels, which it determined to be 26,500 for the total maximum population. This AML was determined to ensure that essential habitat components are present in sufficient amounts to sustain healthy horse and burro populations and healthy range-lands over the long-term, and that the herd size is sufficient to maintain a genetically diverse horse and burro population.

# 10

# Mustangs—Return of the Native or Invasive Species?

*Kerry Kelly*

*Kerry Kelly writes at* Hoofbeats, *a blog about horses hosted at* Chron.com, *the website of the* Houston Chronicle.

*Horses are native to North America. However, they appear to have gone extinct thousands of years ago and were only reintroduced with the European invasion of the continent. Some argue that horses are natives and should be protected as such. Others argue that horses are feral invaders driving away natives. Neither of these positions is wholly true or false. The federal government, however, has determined to protect wild horse populations, not to try to eliminate them.*

## The Claims

1. Wild horses didn't become extinct in North America and remnants of the ancient herds were still present in this hemisphere when Columbus landed in the New World in 1492.

2. Mustangs on public lands are a feral, invasive species, introduced into an environment where they are not native and should not be allowed to roam.

## The Background

The two claims are at opposite extremes of an ongoing debate that surrounds the federal government's wild horse roundups in the West.

It's generally accepted that horse species evolved on the North American continent. The fossil record for equine-like species goes back nearly 4 million years. Modern horses evolved in North America about 1.7 million years ago, according to researchers at Uppsala University, who studied equine DNA. Scientists say North American horses died out between 13,000 and 10,000 years ago, at the end of the Pleistocene Epoch, after the species had spread to Asia, Europe, and Africa. Horses were reintroduced by the Spanish explorers in the 16th century. Animals that subsequently escaped or were let loose from human captivity are the ancestors of the wild herds that roam public lands today.

That's the theory, but revisionists point out that some sources, including the Book of Mormon and Native American cultural tradition, say horses have been continually present on the continent long after the last Ice Age. Some folks contend the original Appaloosa horses of the Nez Perce tribe, which were distinct from other horses, were a remnant of the original equines of the Americas. Over the years, the horse extinction theory has changed.

---

*Some ranchers call mustangs "long-legged rats."*

---

Many scientists once thought horses died out on the continent before the arrival of the ancestors of the American Indians, but archeologists have found equine and human bones together at sites dating back to more than 10,000 years ago. The horse bones had butchering marks, indicating the animals were eaten by people, according to "Horses and Humans: The Evolution of Human-Equine Relationships," edited by Sandra L. Olsen.

So it appears that humans and horses coexisted in the New World prior to 1492, but did they continue to survive in North America over the last 100 centuries?

The claim that wild horses in America are as invasive as Asian clams in Lake Tahoe or rabbits in Australia also is made in the wild horse management debate. Some ranchers call mustangs "long-legged rats" and reader comments on RGJ [*Reno Gazette Journal*] stories about roundups always include opinions that the mustangs are feral interlopers and should be dealt with as vermin.

Federal law makes the argument academic.

In 1971, Congress declared wild horses and burros to be "*living symbols of the historic and pioneer spirit of the West; (and) that they contribute to the diversity of life forms within the nation and enrich the lives of the American people.*"

Lawmakers unanimously decided the free-roaming equines be "*protected from capture, branding, harassment, or death, and to accomplish this they are to be considered in the area where presently found as an integral part of the natural system of public land.*"

Federal officials are charged with managing the free-roaming herds to achieve an ecological balance, and disagreements about the wisdom and quality of that management is the source of current debates.

## The Verdict

By definition, horses are North American natives because most of their evolutionary development took place on this continent. They are "native" rather than "livestock-gone-loose," because they originated here and co-evolved with the American habitat, according to Jay F. Kirkpatrick, director of the Science and Conservation Center in Billings, Montana.

DNA research by molecular biologist Ann Forsten of Uppsala University concludes the ancient horses and the modern domestic horses are the same species. That finding contradicts critics who maintain the original North American horses and the ones that were reintroduced aren't the same animals.

No one is certain why, at the end of the last Ice Age, equines vanished from the hemisphere. Theories of the cause of the extinction include drought, disease, or a result of hunting by humans. The submergence of the Bering land bridge prevented any return migration from Asia. There's no proof any horses escaped extinction in the Americas. If horses survived in the New World up to the 15th century, then no one has ever been able to find the physical evidence to prove the theory.

But, as horse advocates maintain, modern horses evolved here and that's an adequate reason to consider them native American species, and not "invasive" or "introduced feral animals."

The horses were "reintroduced" to the continent, unlike the Asian clams in Tahoe or the rabbits of Australia, which were inserted into regions where Nature never put them and where they could disrupt the ecological balance.

Truth Meter: Given what we know about the history and evolution of horses in North America, both claims are false.

# Sterile Invasive Plants Can Help Protect the Environment

*Colin Poitras*

*Colin Poitras is a writer at* UConn Today.

*Burning bush is a popular ornamental plant because of its impressive colors. It is also a dangerous invasive, which can spread quickly and damage native plants. A researcher at the University of Connecticut's College of Agriculture managed to create a non-fertile variety of burning bush, which can be sold as an ornamental without spreading. This will be a huge help to sellers of ornamentals, and will also protect the environment.*

Professor Yi Li's laboratory in the University of Connecticut's [UConn] College of Agriculture and Natural Resources has developed a seedless variety of the popular ornamental shrub *Euonymus alatus*, also called 'burning bush,' that retains the plant's brilliant foliage yet eliminates its ability to spread and invade natural habitats.

## Burning Bush

"The availability of a triploid seedless, non-invasive variety of burning bush creates a win-win situation for both consumers and commercial nurseries," says Li, head of UConn's Transgenic Plant Facility and director of the New England Invasive Plant Center at the Storrs campus. "The bush is an extremely

Colin Poitras, "UConn Scientist Develops Sterile Variety of Invasive Plant," *UConn Today*, August 19, 2011. Copyright © 2011 University of Connecticut. All rights reserved. Reproduced with permission.

popular ornamental plant for landscapers and gardeners because of its intense red autumn foliage and robust ability to grow in a wide range of soils and environmental conditions. In addition, the plant has very few pest or disease problems."

Also known as 'winged euonymus' because of its distinctive winged branches, burning bush is a top cash crop for the $16 billion ornamental plant industry. It is especially popular in New England and along the eastern seaboard, where the shrub is used for foundation plantings, hedges, and along highways and commercial strips.

National sales of burning bush top tens of millions of dollars each year. The plant, however, spreads aggressively and has been listed as an invasive species in 21 states. It has already been banned in Massachusetts and New Hampshire, and is on an invasive plant 'watch list' in many other states, including Connecticut.

The economic cost of invasive plants is estimated at more than $40 billion per year in the U.S.

The creation of a non-invasive variety of burning bush should help restore the shrub's prominence in the commercial marketplace.

---

*Developing sterile, non-invasive* Euonymus alatus . . . *is of great importance to the American ornamental horticulture industry and gardeners.*

---

"This is a big win for everyone," says Bob Heffernan, executive director of the Connecticut Green Industries Council. "We get to keep selling a popular plant, the public gets to keep using it in their landscapes, and the environment is safe from invasives."

## Biologically Sterile, Economically Fertile

Professor Max Cheng, a horticultural plant biotechnologist at the University of Tennessee-Knoxville, says Li's success in regenerating a triploid non-invasive burning bush "has great economic and environmental significance."

"Several universities and laboratories in the U.S. have been working on developing triploid or sterile burning bush for years," says Cheng. "Endosperm cells of angiosperms are naturally triploid, but regeneration from endosperm cells, particularly from endosperms of woody species, is often very difficult. Dr. Li's success represents a major breakthrough in developing sterile, non-invasive *Euonymus alatus*, which is of great importance to the American ornamental horticulture industry and gardeners."

Mark Sellew, the owner of Prides Corner Farms of Lebanon, Conn., one of the largest wholesale nurseries in the eastern U.S., also praised UConn's success in developing a sterile variety of burning bush.

"This sterile cultivar of burning bush could not come soon enough," says Sellew. "This plant is a very important part of my business. We love working with UConn. I think this shows how very important it is for industry and academia to work together."

Burning bush's invasive characteristics stem from its prodigious seed production. The plant produces tens of thousands of seeds that are transported by rainwater and birds to other sites, especially open woodlands, where they create dense thickets that displace native vegetation. The plant's root system forms a tight mat below the soil surface and its broad profile (it averages 6 to 9 feet in height and is capable of reaching 15 feet) creates heavy shade that threatens the survival of plants living beneath it.

Native to eastern Asia, the deciduous *Euonymus alatus* was introduced in the United States around 1860. The shrub's natural ornamental features have been genetically improved over time, giving rise to its widespread popularity. It can be found in the eastern United States from New England to Florida, and as far west as Illinois.

Recognizing the plant's popularity among consumers and its economic importance to the ornamental plant and landscape industries, Li obtained a grant from the U.S. Department of Agriculture in 2003 to work on the development of a non-invasive variety of burning bush. The New England Invasive Plant Center has provided additional funding for the research since 2006. The invasive plant center was made possible through the support of Connecticut Rep. Rosa DeLauro (D-3rd District). DeLauro helped secure federal funding to launch the center, which aims to develop strategies and methods to address invasive plant problems.

The new lines of sterile non-invasive burning bush plant—which were derived from a popular dwarf variety known as (*E. alatus*) 'Compactus'—took years to develop. Members of Li's research team, Chandra Thammina, Mingyang He, Litang Lu, and others, painstakingly removed thousands of immature and mature endosperm from deep inside the plant's seeds under sterile conditions and then treated them with special plant growth regulators. The team carefully maintained endosperm tissue explants in Petri dishes so that a callus, bud, seedling, and ultimately a new triploid seedless variety were grown.

## Patience and Success

"Finding the right combination of plant growth regulators and repeatedly testing and re-testing the process to validate its success was a lengthy, yet ultimately rewarding, process," Li says.

The process to produce triploid plants from endosperm tissues is so difficult that since endosperm regeneration of plants was first reported in the early 1950s, it has been successful in only 32 plant species. Li praises his research team's persistence, dedication, and passion, which, he says, carried his staff through the long hours necessary for separating thousands of mature and immature endosperms once the plants went to seed in the fall.

The research report appears in the August 2011 issue of *HortScience,* an international journal serving horticulture scientists and the horticulture industry.

The research team reports that it successfully produced 12 independently regenerated triploid plants of burning bush. Triploid plants are sterile due to uneven chromosome division as cells multiply. Li is working with UConn's Office of Technology Commercialization to patent the process used to regenerate the burning bush triploid and ultimately bring the new plant variety to the commercial horticulture industry.

# Sterile Invasive Plants Won't Protect the Environment

*Ellen Sousa*

*Ellen Sousa gardens and farms on Turkey Hill Brook Farm in Massachusetts. She is the author of* The Green Garden: The New England Guide to Planning, Planting and Maintaining an Eco-Friendly Garden.

*Scientists, with government funding, are attempting to develop sterile varieties of invasive plants that are used as popular garden ornamentals. The hope is that sterile varieties won't spread and damage the ecosystem. However, historically, sterile varieties often revert to fertile over time. In addition, sterile varieties will take some time before becoming commercially available. Rather than putting money in research on sterile plants, it would be better to educate gardeners about the dangers of invasive ornamentals and work to replace invasive ornamentals with native plant species.*

Were you aware that USDA [US Department of Agriculture] is sponsoring research at the University of Connecticut to develop sterile varieties of Winged Burning Bush (*Euonymus alatus*) and Japanese barberry (*Berberis thunbergii*)—both non-native plants spreading aggressively into natural and agricultural areas in many parts of the USA.

Ellen Sousa, "Developing Sterile Invasives . . . Why Bother?" *Native Plants and Wildlife Gardens*, 2012. Copyright © 2012 Ellen Sousa. All rights reserved. Reproduced with permission.

## Sterile Does Not Stay Sterile

Sounds like a good idea, right? After all, if the plant is sterile—in other words, it doesn't produce viable seeds or berries—it can be safely planted without risk of its seeds being spread by birds (or wind) into other areas. But history shows that this theory hasn't worked well for other ornamental invasives. Sterile cultivars of the invasive purple loosestrife such as 'Dropmore Purple' and 'Morden's Pink' were found to eventually produce viable pollen and seed and happily cross-pollinate with the wild species. Reversion from "sterile" to "fertile" has also been reported in a number of other plants marketed as "sterile," including Bradford/Callery Pear (*Pyrus calleryana*), reported invasive from the Great Lakes south to the Gulf Coast. To quote from [the 1993 film] *Jurassic Park*, "Nature will find a way."

---

*Why invest all the energy and tax dollars into development of plants that shouldn't be growing here in the first place? Simply put, it's about money.*

---

The environmental problems caused by invasive plants spreading from home landscapes is well-known, at least by governmental agencies and ecologists, if not consumers. Both burning bush and barberry have significant negative impacts on natural systems when they grow where they don't belong. Although now banned for sale in many states, including Massachusetts and New Hampshire, introducing sterile cultivars are not the solution. The runaway horse left the barn years ago, and our unmanaged woodlands are now heavily infested.

Where barberry has taken over woodland areas, studies show the plant can alter the soil chemistry (pH) and increase nitrate levels, making the soil inhospitable to existing woodland trees and understory plants who eventually decline along with the associated wildlife that depend on them. The presence of barberry is also being linked with high numbers of

Lyme Disease, a horrible disease now approaching epidemic levels in the northeast. Barberry's thorny foliage is good cover for mice and small rodents, who researchers from the Cary Institute for Ecosystem Studies believe are the top apex of the Lyme Disease pathogen, more so even than deer.

## Economic Incentives

So why do we want to continue the heavy reliance on these plants in the nursery trade? Why invest all the energy and tax dollars into development of plants that shouldn't be growing here in the first place? Simply put, it's about money.

Burning bush sales are said to top $38 million nationwide, and plant breeders will tell you that consumers want this plant, that they ask for it, and the work fulfills a real demand. I understand that a lot of people buy plants on impulse because of their color, or they see a plant in a friend's yard and decide to buy it for their own property without researching it first. But I'm willing to bet that most consumers are willing to take this advice: "*Barberry is a bad choice for the environment. Plant THIS instead.*" In my own experience as a garden coach, I have only had *one* client in 5 years that did not remove their burning bushes after I explained their impact on our natural ecosystems.

I feel quite proud that my advice has led to the removal of a couple of dozen winged burning bush from suburban Massachusetts yards. I believe that landscaping professionals have great power to influence landscaping trends, and we have a responsibility to educate consumers about the consequences of their landscaping choices.

Admittedly, the rich burgundy color of red barberry cultivars . . . are attractive in home landscapes and the birds are happy to eat the berries. But when berries are deposited in nearby woods, seedlings generally revert to the green form, which begin their stealth campaign for understory dominance.

Not all states consider invasive plants as a legislative priority at the moment, but local landscaping and nursery organizations seem to be picking up the slack. The CT Landscape & Nursery Association has implemented a voluntary phase-out of the use of invasive Japanese barberry cultivars (but unfortunately not burning bush), and hopefully other green industry organizations will follow suit.

It also appears that our federal agencies need to re-evaluate where they are devoting their energy. The USDA web site proudly announces that sterile barberry cultivars should be available for sale *within a decade*. OK, but in the meantime, our remaining intact natural support systems are increasingly degraded by the continuing presence of invasives in home and public landscapes.

## Restore Native Plants

We need to persuade our governmental agencies to re-allocate resources to cultivating and restoring native plant populations in our natural areas, not pandering to landscaping trends.

So, for gardeners looking for alternatives to winged burning bush and invasive barberry, what can they plant that offers the same outstanding characteristics without damaging the environment?

There is a native *Euonymus atropurpureus* (Eastern Wahoo) that has the blazing red color of the invasive variety. Other eastern native shrubs with fiery fall foliage are Virginia Sweetspire (*Itea virginica*) and Highbush Blueberry (*Vaccinium corymbosum*).

If you enjoy the architectural shape of burning bush, plant Pagoda Dogwood (*Cornus altinifolia*) or *Amelanchier* shadbush (aka Serviceberry).

For the red/burgundy or gold foliage cherished in the Japanese barberry cultivars, try dark or gold-leafed cultivars of Ninebark (*Physocarpus opulifolius*). . . .

If you're looking for a low thorny hedging plant as living 'barbed wire' to keep unwanted visitors out, try the native Virginia or Carolina Rose (*Rosa virginiana* or *carolina*).

# Organizations to Contact

*The editors have compiled the following list of organizations concerned with the issues debated in this book. The descriptions are derived from materials provided by the organizations. All have publications or information available for interested readers. The list was compiled on the date of publication of the present volume; names, addresses, phone and fax numbers, and e-mail and Internet addresses may change. Be aware that many organizations take several weeks or longer to respond to inquiries, so allow as much time as possible.*

**Center for Invasive Species Management (CISM)**
235 Linfield Hall, PO Box 173120, Montana State University
Bozeman, MT  59717
(406) 994-7862
e-mail: weedcenter@montana.edu
website: www.weedcenter.org

The Center for Invasive Species Management (CISM) is dedicated to supporting land managers; community-based cooperative weed and invasive species management areas; local, state, and federal governments; western regional partners; concerned citizens; and the public in their dealings with invasive species. In pursuit of these goals, it coordinates invasive plant programs, holds conferences, and provides other services. Its website includes news, articles, and fact sheets on invasive species, and educational resources for children and adults.

**Center for Invasive Species Research (CISR)**
Chapman Hall, Room 108A, 900 University Ave.
Riverside, CA  92521
(951) 827-4714
e-mail: cisr@ucr.edu
website: http://cisr.ucr.edu

The Center for Invasive Species Research (CISR) is based on the University of California Riverside Campus and works to manage invasion of exotic pests and diseases in California. It works to develop systematic methodology for dealing with invasives through risk assessment, early detection, eradication measures, and other methods. The Center's website includes articles, blogs, and information on invasive species.

### Conservation International

2011 Crystal Dr., Suite 500, Arlington, VA   22202
(703) 341-2400
website: www.conservation.org

Conservation International's goal is to promote biological research and work with national governments and businesses to protect biodiversity hot spots worldwide. On its website, the organization publishes fact sheets that explain its values, mission, and strategies, as well as news and reports of its successes.

### Environment Canada

351 St. Joseph Blvd., Gatineau, Quebec
  K1A 0H3
(819) 997-2800 • fax: (819) 994-1412
e-mail: enviroinfo@ec.gc.ca
website: www.ec.gc.ca

Environment Canada is a department of the Canadian government. Its goal is the achievement of sustainable development in Canada through conservation and environmental protection. The department publishes reports, fact sheets, news, and speeches, many of which are available on its website.

### Friends of the Earth International (FOEI)

PO Box 19199, Amsterdam   1000 GD
  The Netherlands
+31 20 622 1369 • fax: +31 20 639 2181
website: www.foei.org

Friends of the Earth International (FOEI) is an international grassroots environmental network. Its member organizations campaign worldwide for food sovereignty, economic justice, and biodiversity, among other environmental and social justice issues. Its website includes news releases, reports, and numerous other publications and resources about topics such as biodiversity and the drawbacks of genetically modified crops.

## Greenpeace USA

702 H St. NW, Washington, DC 20001
(800) 326-0959 • fax: (202) 462-4507
e-mail: info@wdc.greenpeace.org
website: www.greenpeaceusa.org

Greenpeace USA opposes nuclear energy and the use of toxic chemicals and supports ocean and wildlife preservation. It uses controversial direct-action techniques and strives for media coverage of its actions in an effort to educate the public. It publishes the quarterly magazine *Greenpeace* and the books *Coastline* and *The Greenpeace Book on Antarctica*. On its website, Greenpeace publishes fact sheets, reports, and articles.

## Intergovernmental Panel on Climate Change (IPCC)

7bis Avenue de la Paix, C.P. 2300, Geneva 2 CH - 1211
   Switzerland
+41 22 730 8208 • fax: +41 22 730 8025
e-mail: IPCC-Sec@wmo.int
website: www.ipcc.ch

The Intergovernmental Panel on Climate Change (IPCC) was established by the World Meteorological Organization (WMO) and the United Nations Environment Programme (UNEP) in 1988. The role of the IPCC is to assess information relevant to understanding the scientific basis of risk of human-induced climate change, its potential impacts, and options for adaptation and mitigation. The IPCC website includes press releases, global climate change reports, links, and publications available for free download.

## National Invasive Species Council (NISC)
1849 C St. NW, Mail Stop 3530, Washington, DC   20240
(202) 208-5978
e-mail: invasivespecies@ios.doi.gov
website: www.doi.gov/invasivespecies

The National Invasive Species Council (NISC) is a government council that provides high-level interdepartmental coordination of invasive species actions and works to address invasive species at the national level in the United States. The NISC oversees implementation of invasive species actions and encourages planning and action at local levels. Its website includes news updates and information on prevention of invasives, detection of invasives, and other issues surrounding invasive species.

## North American Invasive Species Network (NAISN)
e-mail: naisn.coordinator@gmail.com
website: www.naisn.org

The North American Invasive Species Network (NAISN) is a network of government, university, and other organizations and individuals focused on invasive species issues. NAISN compiles national statistics on invasives, coordinates invasive surveillance and tracking, and offers educational seminars, among other services. The website includes information, links, and lists of invasive species.

## US Department of Agriculture (USDA)
1400 Independence Ave. SW, Washington, DC   20250
(202) 720-279
website: www.usda.gov

The US Department of Agriculture (USDA) is the US government department responsible for developing and executing US farm policy. Its website includes news updates, reports, and publications such as *Agriculture Fact Book*.

# Bibliography

## Books

Eric Chivian      *Sustaining Life: How Human Health Depends on Biodiversity.* New York: Oxford University Press, 2008.

Mike N. Clout and Peter A. Williams, eds.      *Invasive Species Management: A Handbook of Principles and Techniques.* New York: Oxford University Press, 2009.

Alfred W. Crosby      *Ecological Imperialism: The Biological Expansion of Europe, 900–1900,* 2nd ed. New York: Cambridge University Press, 2004.

Mark A. Davis      *Invasion Biology.* New York: Oxford University Press, 2009.

Mike Dorcas and John D. Wilson      *Invasive Pythons in the United States: Ecology of an Introduced Predator.* Athens: University of Georgia Press, 2011.

Sylvan Ramsey Kaufman and Wallace Kaufman      *Invasive Plants: Guide to Identification and the Impacts and Control of Common North American Species,* 2nd ed. Mechanicsburg, PA: Stackpole Books, 2012.

Ruben P. Keller, Marc W. Cadotte, and Glenn Sandiford, eds.      *Invasive Species in a Globalized World: Ecological, Social, and Legal Perspectives on Policy.* Chicago: University of Chicago Press, 2014.

Elizabeth Kolbert    *The Sixth Extinction: An Unnatural History.* New York: Henry Holt and Co., 2014.

Jackson Landers    *Eating Aliens: One Man's Adventures Hunting Invasive Animal Species.* North Adams, MA: Storey Publishing, 2012.

Julie L. Lockwood, Martha F. Hoopes, and Michael P. Marchetti    *Invasion Ecology.* Hoboken, NJ: Wiley-Blackwell, 2013.

Kelsi Nagy    *Trash Animals: How We Live with Nature's Filthy, Feral, Invasive, and Unwanted Species.* Minneapolis: University of Minnesota Press, 2013.

Fred Pearce    *The New Wild: Why Invasive Species Will Be Nature's Salvation.* Boston: Beacon Press, 2015.

Daniel Simberloff    *Invasive Species: What Everyone Needs to Know.* New York: Oxford University Press, 2013.

Ken Thompson    *Where Do Camels Belong?: Why Invasive Species Aren't All Bad.* Berkeley, CA: Greystone Books, 2014.

## Periodicals and Internet Sources

Lindsay Abrams    "When Community Favorites Are Actually Invasive Species," *Salon,* August 5, 2013. www.salon.com.

William Y. Brown    "Conserving Biological Diversity,"
Brookings Institution, July 2011.
www.brookings.edu.

Rhett A. Butler    "Invasive Species Worsen Damage
from Hawaii's Storms,"
Mongabay.com, August 22, 2014.
www.mongabay.com.

Kasia    "Asian Carp: The Invasive Species
Cieplak-Mayr Von   Thriving in America's Rivers,"
Baldegg    *Atlantic*, May 23, 2012.

*Economist*    "Invasive Species: Not Weeds," March
28, 2015.

*Economist*    "Invasive Species: Thorny Questions,"
May 25, 2013.

Environmental    "Effects of Climate Change on
Law Institute    Aquatic Invasive Species and
Implications for Management and
Research," US Environmental
Protection Agency, 2008. www.eli.org.

Darryl Fears    "The Dirty Dozen: 12 of the Most
Destructive Invasive Animals in the
United States," *Washington Post*,
February 23, 2015.

Elizabeth Kolbert    "The Big Kill: New Zealand's Crusade
to Rid Itself of Mammals," *New
Yorker*, December 22, 2014.

Katie Langin    "Genetic Engineering to the Rescue
Against Invasive Species," *National
Geographic*, July 18, 2014.

Nicholas Lund          "Thanks for Nothing, New York
                       City," *Slate*, November 17, 2014.
                       www.slate.com.

Emma Marris            "Opinion: It's Time to Stop Thinking
                       That All Non-Native Species Are
                       Evil," *National Geographic*, July 24,
                       2014.

Megan McArdle          "Should Cities Ban Invasive Plants?,"
                       *Daily Beast*, February 8, 2013.
                       www.thedailybeast.com.

Monte Morin            "Invasive Species Get By with a Little
                       Help from Their Alien Friends," *Los
                       Angeles Times*, December 23, 2014.

Frank Nelson           "New Zealand Imports Foreign
                       Workers: Dung Beetles," *Pacific
                       Standard*, October 21, 2011.

Michelle Nijhuis       "How Climate Change Is Helping
                       Invasive Species Take Over,"
                       *Smithsonian Magazine*, December
                       2013.

Darren Orf             "The Battle Against Invasive Species
                       Rages On," *Vox*, April 5, 2012.
                       http://archive.voxmagazine.com.

Fred Pearce            "Invasive Species Will Save Us: The
                       New Ways We Must Think About the
                       Environment Now," *Salon*, April 11,
                       2015. www.salon.com.

Elisabeth              "Answer for Invasive Species: Put It
Rosenthal              on a Plate and Eat It," *New York
                       Times*, July 9, 2011.

Michael Todd    "Not Ready for Prime Time: Making Fuel Out of Invasive Plants," *Pacific Standard*, November 20, 2013.

Carl Zimmer     "Turning to Darwin to Solve the Mystery of Invasive Species," *New York Times*, October 9, 2014.

# Index